POEMS FOR THE END OF THE WORLD

poems by

Suzi Q. Smith

Finishing Line Press
Georgetown, Kentucky

POEMS FOR THE END OF THE WORLD

ACKNOWLEDGMENTS

Thank you to all who helped to make this book possible. Writing this has been strong medicine for me, and I offer them now in hopes that they will also be for you. This book is dedicated to the sweet earth, holding and transforming. To the generous sky, giving and forgiving. To my beloved daughter, who inspires me to love and teaches me more every day. To my family, who enrich my every fiber with grace and laughter. To my grandmother, who first introduced me to poetry and assured me it was worthy of attention. To my mother, who first introduced me to the art of patience, persistence, and tenderness. To my siblings, who make me believe that I can do anything. To my cousins, my nieces, my nephews, to my ever-expanding family. To my generous and kind teachers, mentors, and friends, who encourage and uplift me. To the visionaries and the waymakers, Ashara Ekundayo and Dr. Clarissa Pinkola Estes, whose words have lifted and carried me into new understandings of possibility. To Franklin Cruz and Sheree Brown, the sweet poets who sat with me in gardens on Saturday mornings and gave writing prompts that began some of these poems. To my beloved community, those who have held me as the world ends and begins and ends and begins. I love you.

"Introductions in Green", "How to Make Love", and "The Laughing Barrel Must Have Been Cobalt Blue" first appeared in *The Poets Project at Casa Grande: A Colorado Anthology*. Published 2021 by The Denver Foundation.

"Maybe it's the End of the World and Maybe That's Fine, Maybe That's Fine" first appeared in *Suspect Press*. December 2016.

Publisher: Leah Huete de Maines
Editor: Christen Kincaid
Cover Art: Vogue M. Robinson
Author Photo: Suzi Q. Smith
Cover Design: Elizabeth Maines McCleavy

Order online: www.finishinglinepress.com
        also available on amazon.com

Author inquiries and mail orders:
Finishing Line Press
P. O. Box 1626
Georgetown, Kentucky 40324
U. S. A.

Table of Contents

"What can I do? // One must begin somewhere. // Begin what? // The only thing in the world worth beginning: // The End of the world of course."
—Aimé Césaire

For the rapture. For Y2K. For all the men who broke my heart. For the illnesses. For the recoveries. For the friends who moved away. For the friends who weren't friends. For the fires in the Amazon. In Australia. Colorado. For the Watch Night services. For the ones we said goodbye to. For the ones who left before we got the chance. For the divorces. Mine, yours, theirs.

Especially: for the day after. For the water and its wide waves. For the soil beneath the ashes. For the brave, early grass. For the carrying wind. For the babies and their laughter. For the sleepy parents. For falling in love over and over. For the faith, opening one eye slowly and saying, "Yes." For the courage of sun.

A Song for Red Mornings in Spring

let this be the book of the rooster
of the eastern sky
call of the robin breast
of the drained morning and hoards running
let it be the wind at backs and feet stirring
let it be unstoppable
a wave
a high ground seeking
a knowing
a beginning as much as an end
let the trees fall where they must
flying back behind a flooding ground
an answer of blue sky coming
let me know and keep knowing
trust the hips and feet to move forward even unwavering
let the sun rise and see me soaring
let me be forgiven for all I leave
at my feet for all I cannot carry
or convince
let me keep running
until I get there let me get there.

Introductions in Green

1.   I am going to die. Obviously.
        So are you. We don't know
        when. Or who will go first.
        I'd better tell you everything I think
        I know or remember while I am still
        alive.

2.   These are my hieroglyphs.
        I hope you can use them. Some of them
        are recipes. Some of them are prescriptions.

3.   Most are only moments
        I still have questions about
        or stones I wanted to squeeze
        before I skipped them
        into a deep lake.

4.   Probably, this is the lake.
        And the stones. And my hands.
        The ripples on the surface of the water
        as the stones skitter across.
        The fish. The flies. Mosquitos.
        If there are ducks, this is them too.

5.   Maybe in the future,
        you won't know what a duck is.

        Maybe I should learn to draw
        a bird that flies and floats and stretches

        its long neck into water while
        its body is perfectly still atop the depths.

6.   Sometimes, when the sun hits just right,
        the green in their feathers looks like emeralds
        or spray painted metal, a treasure.
        It almost doesn't look real.

7. A treasure.

8. Do you believe the wild and
    precious imagination of God?
    I hope you imagine
    something beautiful for God
    in return.

9. You are precious, you know?
    You are alive for now.
    I do not know if this will still be true
    when you read this, but so am I.

10. So many of our beloveds
    have not survived.
    Still: we are here,
    brave enough to have
    beloveds.

11. Sometimes I close
    like a fist and that, too,
    is love.

12. I exist. Therefore, I deserve to be loved.

13. I am learning to stop
    apologizing for declaring my own
    deservedness for love.

14. Everything alive needs love.
    Even the things with thorns.
    Even the thorns.
    Even the blood dripping
    from fingertips into the soil.
    Yes, even the finger.
    Yes, even the soil.
    The worms, dancing in the dark of it.

How to Make Love

If you want someone to know that you love them, go to the local butcher. Buy the best whole chicken they have, organs and all. Go to the market with the best produce and buy a few onions, yellow enough to make you hungry, a few shallots maybe two hands full. A heavy box of kosher salt. A pound of carrots so orange they sing, a stalk of celery crisp as winter. A quart of heavy cream thick as a cow's shoulder. A bottle of brandy or cognac, depending on what you like. A bundle of bay leaves, fresh if you can find them. A pound of butter. You should already have several cloves of garlic on hand at home, we are talking about love after all, but it might be wise to add a few more to your basket if you feel like it's time.

Now we all have our own methods, but I feel like it's best to sing on your way home, and while you're preparing the ingredients. I prefer Anita Baker and Donny Hathaway for this part, and, of course, Stevie Wonder, but do you. Chop the yellow onions while you sing. Crying may also occur. Best to leave the onions in irregular pieces, let your love know that you chopped them yourself. Cut the carrots into fat coins, then again in half if you feel like it. Wash the celery down to its base, all between the ribs where the dirt likes to hide. I hope I didn't have to tell you to wash everything else: your onions, your carrots, your hands.

I like a heavy knife for all this chopping, but work with what you got. You don't need good knives to love somebody, but it helps. What you do need is a stockpot big enough to hold a whole chicken and all these vegetables, plus some water. You should have a cast iron skillet too, but it's alright if you ain't that grown yet. Best to rinse the pot, it probably has some dust or grease on it from sitting on top of the fridge or under the sink, or where ever you pull it out from. Now, on low heat, pour a little olive oil and let it warm. After about half a song, add your chopped vegetables to the pot and let them spend some time together under a lid. When they start to feel a little soft, stir them with a wooden spoon. I hope you have a wooden spoon.

As for the chicken, if you haven't worked with a whole chicken before, the organs are probably inside it. You'll need to reach in between its legs and pull them out. This might sound nasty, and it might even be nasty, but it's got to be done and if you can't handle a little nasty, you might not be ready to fall in this type of love yet. Set the organs aside, we'll do something with them in a little while. Don't let the juices spill onto the counter, put them on a plate or in some type of container. Cover them and put them in the fridge, I'll tell you another time how to make pâté.

Now that your chicken is ready for cooking – you washed it, didn't you? We talked about this. Wash everything. Pray however you pray. I give thanks for all my food (especially if something had to die). I thank my food, the land it grew on, the people who raised it, who slaughtered or harvested it. You ever think about how many hands and lives are involved on your plate? That's a lot of thank-yous. Thank the chicken while you wash its body, while you go all between its legs and pull its organs out, thank it when you put it in the pot on top of the semi-soft vegetables, stirred by a wooden spoon. Let the chicken sit on top of the onions, the carrots, the celery on low heat and under a lid. Let the steam help them get together and fall in proper love for the length of two or three Nina Simone songs, checking in between.

Now, of course, we need to add water. Nothing good can grow without water. Some folks will tell you to use filtered water, which is good if you got it, but if we come to the kitchen with clean hands and a pure heart, we can make the best out of what we have and tap water will do just fine. Add enough water for the chicken to be cooked entirely, enough to let it rise to the top. Now you'll want to add a couple of bay leaves, or more if you like (here is where we must listen to our own blood), a half palm of kosher salt, depending on the size of your hands.

Let all of this roll into a soft boil, then bring the heat back down to low and walk away for an hour or so. This is a good time to do laundry, but probably not to read because it is too easy to get lost inside a book and forget to take the chicken out. When the chicken is cooked (and I mean falling-off-the-bone cooked, not a shade of pink nowhere), bring it onto a plate and let it cool. It might fall apart in this process, don't panic. We're about to take it apart anyway, so go ahead and bring it out in pieces if you got to.

Keep the broth on low low very low heat. When the chicken is cool enough for you to touch without cussing, pull the skin off the meat and the meat off the bones. Put the meat aside (in a container, then into the fridge) and add the skin and bones back into the pot. We're gonna let these bones cook slow for a long time, all night, so you can go ahead and read now if you want to and come back to this tomorrow.

When you wake up, your whole house should smell like somebody loves you. There might be a layer of gel and fat on the top of your broth. You're welcome. Now you'll strain the broth into another pot. With the bones and skin and bay leaves and vegetables boiled lifeless all looking at each other in the strainer, you have compost that wants to spend time in your soil. We don't believe in wasting anything in this kitchen. Add this mixture to your compost bucket if you got one, or go ahead and start one in an old coffee can. Keep your broth on the stove, bring it back to a low boil and add some rice. You washed it, right? I know I didn't tell you to buy rice but you should already have some – if you don't even have rice, I don't know if you should be trying to cook love dishes just yet. Let the rice cook itself soft as you like it, and add the chicken from yesterday back into the pot and let it get warm.

Now I know this sounds easy, chicken and rice soup. But if you do all this for your intended and they don't fall in love? You deserve better. And at least now you know how to cook.

Mezzo Sopranos Get the Sad Songs

Did you hear the one about the long lines around
the gun shop and the sold out bullets
and the empty grocery store shelves in the United States?
What will happen when our lights are out?

I hope we sing like the people in Italy.
I only really know two arias, one of which is "Lascia Te Mi Morire"
                                        translation: *bring me my death*
so I don't think I'll sing that one,

but I'll tell you this:
I'll sing before I shoot,
I'll sing before I shoot,
ain't never been afraid of heaven anyhow.

Maybe it's the End of the World and Maybe That's Fine, Maybe That's Fine

I.   The Good Old Days

"See, in the good old days this doesn't happen, because they used to treat them very, very rough. And when they protested once,   *you know, they would not do it again so easily."*

"You see, in the good old days, law enforcement acted a lot quicker than this, a lot quicker. In the good old days, they'd rip   *him out of that seat so fast."*

"We're not allowed to punch back anymore. I love the old days — *you know what they used to do to guys like that when they were*   *in a place like this? They'd be carried out on a stretcher, folks."*

-Donald J. Trump, campaigning for President of the United States

II.   To-Do List: Preparing to Live in Trump's America
✓   ~~Apply for your concealed carry permit~~. No, violence will not solve this – they will always have more of it than you.
✓   Make sure your daughter, your nieces, all of your darlings have access to birth control and a long-term plan – either not to have children, or to raise an unflinching army of them.
✓   Double-check health insurance – will we still have it? For how long?
✓   Learn your medicine. Take care of your teeth and bones and blood. You will need to sharpen them all.
✓   ~~Buy a gun. Buy several guns.~~ No, now is the time for prayer – it is the only weapon that will work. They will always have more guns and they love the way your insides look when you wear them out.
✓   Have you eaten today? Food made by hands that love your mouth? You must remember to eat.
✓   Breathe. Breathe again.
✓   ~~Steady your shoulders and practice your aim~~. No, remember the order of succession: President, Vice President, Speaker of the House …

✓ Make something honest with your body every day.
   o An ark.
   o An afro.
   o A dress.
   o A song.
   o A stew.
   o A poem.
   o A prayer.
   o A spell.
   o A belt.
   o A slingshot.
   o A howl.
   o A hurricane.

✓ Gather your tribes. Remember the places you have created to exist together; the landscapes in your chest where all of their names are written, the ledges within them offering you shelter. They are all still there. This is still the world.

✓ Breathe. Breathe again.

III. *"We will be ourselves and free, or die in the attempt. Harriet Tubman was not our great-grandmother for nothing."*
           – Alice Walker

I have survived the good old days.
I have survived my own memories.
I have survived 37 Colorado winters.

I have survived poverty and its shame.
I have survived a thousand closed doors and cages.
I have survived my choices.

I have survived seventh grade fights, bad hair, and awkward clothes.
I have survived the girl who called me a nigger bitch when that boy liked me better.
I have survived beauty.

I have survived marriage.
I have survived bodies, in mine and out.
I have survived my own attempts at murder.

I have survived divorce.
I have survived men who pretend to know more about God than
I do.
I have survived phony gods.

I have survived unexpected knocks at the door and uninvited
telephone calls.
I have survived the police.
I have survived the reasons I have called police.

I have survived America.
I will survive this.
I will survive this.

The Laughing Barrel Must Have Been Cobalt Blue

Under the shadow of a headline
looking too much like our children,
we tucked and folded and gathered
ourselves and each other into the
skirt of my grandmother's dining room
tablecloth, all of us lamenting and
listing the labors and losses, the
table spilling over with stories of
the times the police were called
or not called but came, the last
jobs or second interviews, the neighbor
or grocery store clerk, the child
at school and/or their mother and/or
their father and/or the teacher and

the table, listening, dipped in the
center near to snapping under the
burden until my grandmother
emerged from the kitchen, apron
speckled *"but here is the thing,*
the real thing," her pointed finger
stern and scolding us into silence,

"would any of you ever want to be
anything other than what you are?"

and we sat
stunned, staring at ourselves
until we began to laugh

and we laughed
we laughed into each other's shoulders,
we laughed into howling, howled
into howling until the moon herself
walked into the room
staggering, crook'd finger in the air,
laughed her round face into our laughter,

howling a perfect mirror
our moon eyes spilling throaty and harmonious
looking and laughing and loving our rich and
delicious lives too perfect, too precious,
and we ate to music we ate without muting
our tears rolling into our open mouths.

the found women

after Lucille Clifton

i know their names
beloved and tender
these women i walk with
we gather each other bustling
bountiful skirt bottoms held together
in fists, bounding up stairs
blistering with laughter jauntily,
jauntily, i know their names
our soft arms swinging and crookt
hooked into each others' elbows
sweating swapping stories i have joined
the tables of women who labor
who suck and chew the marrow who
laugh and joke into our beer who
rowdy howl in alleyways and gardens
we gang we team we laid proper now
found and finding ourselves
we grow thicker every day
i know their names, sticky thunderous
chorus each others' days
make our tables round with bounty
sweep ghosts out of doors
grease scalps bring stew
make medicine raise babies
gather ourselves and each other
i know our names
we salve salvation delicious
we ripe round juicy bursting joy
we sharp arrows straight aim
we women we sistren we laugh
we love
ourselves
and you
we found
and finding

each other
we still
got plenty
of room.

Ocotillo

When a seed is planted
or buried, abandoned to the soil
it may not know
this is a gift.

> yes, sis, cry. wail. moan.
> tear your hair and gnash your teeth.
> alladat.
> then wash the dishes.

For much of the year, Ocotillo appears to be
an arrangement of large spiny dead sticks.
With rainfall, the plant becomes lush with green leaves.
When water is scarce, the leaves turn brown and fall off.

> every earth-cracked thirsty
> yearning is a seed.
> plant it.
> let it crane toward the sun and bloom.

> > do seeds (the small ones – say, mustard)
> > get jealous or pray to become bigger seeds?
> > do they ever wish they could fill themselves up with air?
> > is that how they imagine growth?

> sometimes i press my fingers
> toward the invitation of sky and say yes.
> bend my face to the sun and laugh,
> remembering how i once clung to the shell i believed was me.

With rain, we find Ocotillo
swelling, blooming open into
bloodshot flowers, earning it the name
"desert coral".

> girl, braid your hair or
> wrap it up and go,

even weeping if you must,
somewhere the sun will touch your face.

The hummingbird, migrating
through the long desert,
relies upon the flowers
of the ocotillo for honey nectar.

did you forget? the kindness of wind and its longing for your skin?
the unrepentant gaze of desert sky?
the rivers that open their mouths to your sorrows,
ready to carry them some place you don't need to go?

i reimagine myself daily.
i abandon old wounds to the soil
until they fertilize it. everything,
even waste, has a purpose.

Ocotillo can grow up to 20 feet tall,
some say they can live over 100 years.

yes, sis, live.
let your bare feet sink into the mud.

i have been afraid
and filled with air before;
did not know i was a small, hard world
becoming large as i unfold.

and i will tell you
and i will tell me (i forget and forget my way)

what is sweeter than longing
for loose, escapable soil
is to be rooted in rock, becoming
honey on a tender tongue.

Outdoor Education for Inner-City Kids

in Denver
every public school student
goes to Balarat Outdoor Education
in fifth grade

which includes
a night walk down a mountain path
we are meant to walk
alone

when I went
I was afraid of the dark
or the mountain lions
or whatever the dark might have held

my best friend Julia and I decided
that which ever of us went first
would wait on the path
for the other

I don't remember now
which of us went first
or who waited for whom
but I do remember we kept our word

that we walked
most of that dark stretch
still frightened
together

When Even the Rivers are Burning

I told my best friend to plant me in the back yard of someone who loves me.
Wrap me in a blanket under a tree so I can still feed something.
I don't need to be right all the time.
In my mind, I have robbed nearly every bank I have entered.
Gunless and charming with a smile and a note.
Have murdered at least a handful of people, some slowly, some quickly.
Some on repeat.

I am in the practice of burying my need to be liked.
I dig it up again most of the time.
Humor so sharp it unearths when I call.
Laugh at myself for mourning things I've never had.
I do not want to waste my life. I do not want to waste my death.
I told my daughter the other day that I don't plan to survive her.
I meant it.

I claim a future as a quiet living thing, a mountain at night.
I want to find a beautiful heaven.
A blissful revolution. A melted metal.
A water clean enough to drink.
A peace to wrap around us all in a welcome welcome welcome.
Find some crisp air to rest inside of.
This hand of God has always been my home.

I'm a stranger everywhere I go.
Grateful to be a welcome guest, begging when I am not.
My daughter and I have decided not to survive the apocalypse.
We know how to surrender. We know how to change.
Of course I feel like the earth.
A mother who knows herself and cares only about her children.
Who wants to feed, even when hungry.

How to Grieve

when you are ready to begin,
look for something alive
something new
and opening.
bend your hand
around the flame of this tender joy
and let it light your way.

place bare feet on the ground.
kneel.
press knees forward.
sit back on feet.
stretch arms up over head.
press forward.
fold into the earth.
forehead, palms.
all touching the naked dirt.

turn head to the side and press left ear to the ground.
listen.
turn head again, press right ear to the ground.
listen.

stretch body flat out pressing chest into the tender
or even frozen soil and lay there, heart open,
arms stretched wide to either side,
fingers curled like claws and grasping,
clawing, digging.

let the earth remind you of how much
voice you've swallowed and feel it
well up in your throat.

wail when you're ready.
moan like the wounded animal you are.
pound your fists against whatever earth is still holding you
and howl the names of all that has been taken from you.

call their names up from the mossy well they have been nearly forgotten in.
claw them up and back to you.
know that you are theirs. they are yours.
hold them.

open your arms wide enough for your shoulder blades
to touch and wing again.
become an open door and let the light move through you.

become yourself again,
these found now treasured bones,
unburied and blessed.

let us weep at the reunion of self and self
and hold.

let us braid ourselves back together.

let our prayers be remembered and heard.

let us become ourselves again.
let us become each other's again.
healed, whole, beloved.

Here's What I Know

how small a world is when dying
or falling
or recovering
or pulling the edges of a knowledge
strewn about among the weeds

I love the weeds
the way they survive and flower
I blow wishes against their seeds
and spread

I love the way
the real ones come thru
with open doors and made plates
I dance like an earthworm emerging in a spring storm

I love the ladybug I saw move among the leaves
escaping the spinning blade I was approaching with
the ladybug spared me from killing it

and let me see myself

not kill it

and already I loved the ladybug
and especially now

I love it more.

Let It Let

pressing weight into grief
weight into weight
a trap
  door perhaps pressing my way
into the crack the in between stone
rolling surrender to the potential of its crushing
or my own strength
or miracle of movement

maybe a door opens
collapses into my breath
and aren't we all quite bored with tears
especially small ones
selfish ones
that have my heart running scared

the small close droplets are the ones that make you crazy
the echo of those unwept howlings
the ting of a valve until it stops

let the blood come rushing back into feeling
let even the boring tears fall
even the predictable flurries
even the most self pitiable
even the small small blood
the bitter and petty shameful

let it let
let myself surrender to the river
to the ocean
let me become water
let me hold only what is mine to hold
let it root and flourish
let the rest drown
let me remember surviving it
as I watch it wash away

The Illness of Spring 2020

99.5
"I'm fine,
after the shower my skin burned.
Might got a touch of that Yung Rona but I'm good,
don't worry about me, I worked out today and everything."
I sweat past fever past illness past past
drink ginger drink vinegar drink broth
take B and C and D and zinc
elderberry nettle irish moss
pineapple ashwaganda

100   for two days, then gone
I slept and slept
cough came and came
head weighted piercing
sweated cleanly into
and through my sheets
so many days I still dance
through and against coughing breaks.

100.5
People send videos and voice messages.
Conspiracies about where the virus came from,
what "they don't want you to know" about cures,
how to blow dry up your nostrils and hop on one foot.
Why black people can't get it.
Why it's killing black people first,
as if I don't already write about the tortured history of
black people and medicine.
As if my black grandmother didn't work as a surgical tech for 30 years,
as if she didn't raise me washing my hands.

101   for two days, then returned
As if I don't already know the ins and outs of illness and conspiracies.
As if I haven't been my own primary caregiver for years.
So I don't tell them I'm sick.
The last thing I want is their suggestions

or to use my small energy calming their fears,
I know how to navigate illness.

101.5   for three days, then gone
I mean, I feel like I got a belt wrapped around my lungs
but I have rapped on stage in a corset more than once.
I'm good, haven't my lungs known wisdom and vice
enough to surrender to breath?
Surrender I know well enough
to text my daughter somewhere in the midst of it.

102   for one week, then returned
". . . if it should get bad,
I'll let you know.
And if it gets really really bad,
you're my beneficiary
and everything I have is yours.
Not to be morbid.
You already know the passcode to my phone."

We have both been through enough
not to cry about this,
to trust wisdom for now and save theatrics
for a more reasonable quiet.

I hope I did enough with my life.
(I still got plenty to do)
I hope I loved hard enough
(I might have loved too hard –

so hard I got distracted from my work,
which is another kind of love,
a less specific all-god's-children kind of love,
burns longer, quieter, enough to light another fire.)

Maybe I got too caught up frivolous and focused
on a single man's cheek bones or voice, hands,

whistling him in and around my thoughts
and probably wasting precious time.

Maybe I should have loved myself harder?
Or scooped my flesh out by my own hands full
offering it to every passerby?
Are cannibals god's children too?

I fall asleep every night curled up with a question
but at least I have insurance and money in the bank.
If there are still banks tomorrow.
If there is still tomorrow.

I go back and forth writing about myself
in past and present tense.

Freedom is Essential

Before the pandemic hit, I bought:
bronzer for the sun kissed look i only really have in summer.
Sterile, single-use vials of imitation tears
Gel pens in blue, black, and red.

In my wish list:
sundresses for a vacation that has since been canceled
dresses so bright and loud they call the kind of attention I only love occasionally
dresses I might not ever wear in the city I call home.

Now that I am so alone
I move my body in ways I never might if I were seen.
I praise my own capacity to know what is dope and divine
without ever needing to be taught.

Strangers who want to feel known by me
have locked me in uncomfortable embraces
and have placed (or tried to place their hands)
in my hair (as a compliment, I am told)

and oh, how they demand their freedom to do so!

Demand to see themselves be seen
glaring at a masked face in a grocery store
or a video turned off in a meeting,
believe they are owed the performance of a smile and submission.

How else do we measure our value
if not our ability to affect each other?
How else do we escape ourselves
if not our ability to absorb each other or drown?

Essential businesses in my city includes of course liquor stores,
marijuana dispensaries, gun stores (which I hear are mostly sold out).
People howl at night to say: I am alive. I am here.
I am still able to affect people around me.

Here, in this body, for nearly a month,
have been all the symptoms of the illness.
I could howl. I say yes to all the unwelcome hugs,
hair touching, and boundless line stepping.

Maybe I am a carrier.
Maybe I am a cure.
Haven't more than a handful of eyes
already decided how best to dissect me?

I mean I'm good
at sheltering in place
and wild grateful
for this sanctified stillness.

Except.
I write out the words every day:

I'm so sorry for your loss
love to you and your family
I'm here
how can I help
what do you need
I'm sorry I'm sorry I'm sorry I'm sorry I'm sorry I'm sorry I'm sorry I'm sorry
I'm sorry I'm sorry I'm sorry I'm sorry I'm sorry I'm sorry I'm sorry I'm sorry
I'm sorry I'm sorry I'm sorry I'm sorry I'm sorry I'm sorry I'm sorry I'm sorry
I'm sorry I'm sorry I'm sorry I'm sorry I'm sorry I'm sorry I'm sorry I'm sorry
I'm sorry I'm sorry I'm sorry I'm sorry I'm sorry I'm sorry I'm sorry I'm sorry
I'm sorry I'm sorry I'm sorry I'm sorry I'm sorry I'm sorry I'm sorry I'm sorry
I'm sorry I'm sorry

If we are lucky, our bodies will teach us the glory of pause
before we die.
We become who we love without the burden of an audience.
We dance into our little bodies hopeful to be loved in and beyond them.

A Guide: How to Move Back Into Your Body

1.   To move back into your body, you must begin by remembering
the nests and caves that you have carved your name on. Every
home you have hidden in. You must remember all that you have
left there and ask it to return. Your body is the only geography.
It will know the way.

2.   Call your names to the winds. All of your names. The ones that
belong to you. The ones that your skin still remembers wearing.
Keep calling the names until they sing. They will sing. Answer
them yes. Press your tongue flat, open your mouth and sing, yes.
It is the only answer one can give in times like these.

3.   When your voice begins to vibrate against the tight drum of your
throat, when it rattles against your teeth and your cheekbones
quiver, plant your feet and spread your arms, and learn to breathe.

4.   Feel the tips of your fingers throb and hum with their new,
pregnant morning. Clap your hands against your thighs and
dance to the resounding echo of your sonorous plump. Eat.
Drink. Laugh until you are music again. Name each moving
part yes. Call the name yes until they open.

5.   Breathe. Be a hymn for each dawn's dew. Be a sweet whisper, yes.

6.   You were once a single drop of water fleeing a dry, hungry
tornado, but you will soon see that you are a swallower of storms.
That is the grumble in your belly. Say yes.

7.   Somewhere inside your body (in your belly button, perhaps,
or lodged deep in your throat) lies the only key you have ever
needed to free yourself. Dive into the sunless and press the dark
until it opens, revealing itself against your electric fingers. It is
there. I promise.

WWJS

My stepfather taught me to shoot when I was 10 years old.
My feet were aching, walking through the woods
wearing my mother's boots, which I had already
outgrown. I longed for wings.
We were, of course, hunting birds.

He taught me not to drag the guns.
He warned me about the kick.
I steadied my stance and shot into a tree trunk.
We didn't shoot any birds that day.
I've still never seen a pheasant.

My sister took me to the range and taught me to shoot a semi-automatic.
She told me most people shoot too high at first,
a reflex of hesitation. It's normal, she tells me.
I aimed. Hit my target with an accuracy so unflinching
we were equal parts proud and frightened.

In my family, there are preachers and soldiers.
I have loved men with scars left by bullets.
Is it the ghosts or the guns that make me an American?
Shooting is a pastime.
Like church.

In high school, I went camping
with my best friend's youth group.
We made our tents, rafted the white waters, built a fire, sang about Jesus.
We took turns shooting pistols and a rifle at some jars and cans in the distance.
We were the Lord's Army.

We are holy and holey.
Faith shaking like a hand that just hit its mark
and that mark is a person with a name and a story
and maybe we are all too haunted to notice
how quickly we flash into ghost.

Haven't we needed to frighten men from our homes?

My mom used to sleep with a gun under her pillow.
I use prayer like my grandmother taught me
and it works in the sense that I have not been murdered
so far.

Becoming Memory

what is a face
but a flash of light?
a life.
fragile, fierce, temporary.
death comes as a thief in the night
and sometimes our bodies thrash against it
and sometimes the bell rings too early,
undressed faces
still finding their shape.

you can tell by the smile
whether or not a person
has been loved
correctly
at least once
which is, of course, too small,
a flame not enough to warm hands
but a spark enough to start a fire.

even the most rapturous fire
is temporary.
even howling, it is going to die.
even in death,
we remember at least flashes,
at least light.

An Open Letter to Those Who Would Come for My Joy

Here.
Have it.
Take as much as you need.
I'm saying.
You need it.
I got it.
I'm making more.

Watch:
In the oven window, the biscuits rising.
You smell that?
Stir this honey into the butter.

See?
You ain't got to steal from me.
My joy laughs at anybody who thinks she don't know her address.
She comes home stumble-drunk and laughing, full of stories every time.

You got your own joy.
She and my joy are friends already.
They play in the sprinklers and braid each other's hair every Thursday.
They shout compliments to each other across streets:

Girl, you wearin that dress!
Don't hurt nobody!

The choreography they made up in middle school
still gets busted out on dance floors like it's 1990-something
until they fall into each other,
out-of-breath laughing.

Look:
These biscuits are ready.
Get you a plate.
Later, I'll teach you how to make them.

Aunties Always Know

sometimes my ancestors
holler
right in my ear

"girl if you don't go get you some joy!"

and i will,
i will.

i want to know joy
this well, this body full of
yes, please and thank you
this blessed rain
let it pour over my upturned face
right into my mouth.

really been in the desert though.
this really been a love drought though.
of course i'm thirsty.

ashamed at all i have drunk
that was not water.

When I Am Free

Assume there was never a plan for my freedom
I hold my hands out, open palmed,
snap off each finger and say:
Here. Eat.
Laugh, fear brings out the mob in people.
An unsheathed ear.
An unleashed fear.
An opening, unveiled mirror.

I'm not claiming to be any type of Messiah.
Who knows loneliness better than a free-drawn clear breath?
I shatter whole buildings that would have me bend to enter
and imagine myself free:
An arrow with wings
who shot herself
into the sky,
piercing and open,
a radical act of love for air
and night and blue and speed.

What is freedom but a devotion to opening?
A madness unconfined?
A clear note played long and wet?
A soft landing in soft black soil?

When I am free
(and here I sing ooooo and leap into a holy ghost dance)
When I am free
(and here even the angels laugh with me in my delight)
When I am free
honey, you have never heard such a hallelujah,
nectar never tasted so sweet.

How to Repent

Self, I have sinned
against you. Sometimes
I think the thoughts I think
are not even yours.

I feel unholy. Let strangers
with dirty hands expect things
from your mouth and probe
for mirrors and cavities,

chastised you
for the traces of them
in each compacted vertebrae,
each bend of spine aching to hold itself;

Self, I have not hollered your name
all the times that I meant to,
gave you no means to find your way home,
I have not prayed in a long time.

Self, I have been afraid to be alone with you.
I wonder if you have gone wild,
if you have lived among the bears,
if they have taught you teeth and claw.

I have bullied you into believing
that our fears are more than shadows.
Will we know ourself again in this new
howl, will we call it God?

Self, I have not always held you as hallowed.
Self, I chopped off your feet and cursed you for crying out.
Self, I laid flat in the river and came up thrashing with a mouthful of fish,
I know it must have been you.

Self, I did not see you.
Self, I did not want to see you.

Self, I am sorry.
Self, I will sin again

and will be sorry then too.

Flirting With Heaven

"what
a fool,"
i think to myself sometimes
so i love
the work
faithful
stays steady as light.

does the sun know
the moon is a pale mirror?
laughs
the sun
does not even
see
the moon

but i am an ocean
lifting my skirts
at its every turn

it winks at me,
i wave and still.

it turns,
i spin into cloud,
fill the skies with mud-thick storm
to hide my shame.

it's a shame
how well i build a hurricane.

can a hurricane swallow the moon?
i once tried to answer this.
my own love
so seismic
i could not see
i was

alone.

what a fool
i feel sometimes,

so shapeless and reaching
for sun.

I Used to Bite when I Was Little

Do you see my face split into smile?
Every crease, a debt I am owed.

Watch:
I open my mouth
clean over the top of my head,
shimmy out my skin.

You feel that hair outstretched
on the back of your neck?
That chill straightening your spine?
The hair on your arms raising?
That's me, collecting.

Come closer.
You can smell the God on my breath.
Honey, *laughs*, I can't even remember
how many times I have died and come back.
Walk between worlds so smooth they are inseparate.

Do you hear that siren howling?
Does it ask you also to forget my name?
Buff the calluses from my feet?
Sweep my wet clay footprints
on my way out the door? Or yours?

My blood knows my voice.
Been opened enough to know how to hunt and gather my sharps into a
salve of body.
Split and spilt into a daughter.
Softed into mother.
Scabbed back into wondrous scraps.

My rugged feet sing salvage yard.
Fluent in fertilizer.
Hunger always finds its way in the dark.
Haven't I died a thousand times?

Imagined myself as light screaming back into this dense and tiny knuckle?

Haven't I made myself a map of whispers?
Don't I chant my way snatching
say:
> this is mine this is mine
> I am mine I am mine
> my name is mine my name is mine

Gleaming
forgive as a form of erasure
breathe in out
I'm a til-you-do-right-by-me
type of miracle.

One day,
my great grandchildren
will stroke your bones tenderly
as they tell the story of your
self-destruction.

Do you hear that?
This empire of broken dog teeth snapping the bone?

How to Find Water

follow the first tear
fallen on cracked desert[1]
find its river
and know water again

cover skin in the mud
in celebration
of skin
and especially mud

love the feet
and the water[2]
and the opening of sky
even the crust that has formed on your heels

love the last tear
of this dry heat journey
if it leads you here
if it brings you water[3]

---

1 here, in this poem, the desert is my heart
howling with wind and ghosts

surely not properly watered
which is fine, I respect a desert
it knows how to survive even when it looks dead
playing dead is, of course, a survival skill

----

2 but here, I also remember
when it was a jungle

hot and wet and living
the singing could be heard for miles

----

3 here, of course, my tears are rain
I, alone, stopped them

aren't we all
just trying to live?

Reflections in Yellow-Gold-Orange-and-Even-Sometimes Red

1. do you know
    as a child
    my hair was
    the color of
    gold? a tiny
    lion's afro?

2. A lion, beaming playful as summer afternoon,
    stretching forepaws in the sun,
    sweet feathers stuck
    to the blood drying on its cheeks,
    yawning wide-mouthed,
    still hungry.

3. We, wounded, press
    tongues flat away
    from the roofs
    of our mouths
    let the breaths soar
    and the voice grow
    fat and wide
    the heads of marigolds
    spilling from our throats,
    buttery petals,
    bursting.

4. Hot water cornbread says come into this kitchen
    and bite before it's cool before it's gone
    claim your piece in teeth prints, leave the
    whole world knowing where your
    mouth has been.

5. My brother was born with something called jaundice
    somebody told me it meant he looked yellow
    and then another time another somebody called me yellow
    (you should know that around here,
    yellow

is sometimes
a shade
of brown).

6.   My sister's eyes are brown
flecked with gold,
a stone dug from the inside
of a mountain.

7.   For two days running,
the barista with the warm smile
and half-hearted beard
has shaped a heart in the foam
of my golden latte,
asking if my order is for here
(again). This is a version of love.

8.   My love, a ginger warm musk.
Turmeric rice with yellower onions.
Sweet plantains frying in coconut oil.
The can of Café Bustelo resting on the counter.
Lemon cleaner bouncing in droplets.

9.   Exhale audibly, tongue out.
They call that lion breath.

10.   I have made friends with all the dandelions in the yard
at the park at the neighbors everywhere
everywhere these days they even smile back at me
when I say good morning.
I love the way dandelions survive and flower.
I blow wishes against their seeds and spread.

11.   I went to the grocery store
and bought beets: red, gold,
orange, all the size
of human hearts.

12.   Skin burnt Colorado sunrise.
        Velvet rich, thick enough to hold a finger print.
        Go from light to dark to light with a trace.
        Roasted. Rooted. Rooting.
        The quiet emergence of morning. The urgency of day.

13.   We have hands that hold the sun. See?
        We made something beautiful today.
        It asked us for everything. We gave it.
        A seed, surrendered to the soil. Tucking a child into bed.
        It gave us something back.

14.   The aging edges of a photograph,
        time rests against neck and shoulders easy,
        an old love whose mattress knows the trace of your body
        and holds it there. A bookmark.
        A key tucked under a flower pot. A nickname. An address.
        A tree you might still be able to climb.

The Air is Dry Here

Obviously I fantasize
about other lives/lands
where I am not asked to leave at least
half of myself (and Of Course the half
of myself that loves myself) quietly
d(r)ying out on the back porch
I dream of oceans and islands
the strong arms of beautiful men
with clean, dark eyes
and (At Least) one of them saying to me
Welcome Home.

In the Beginning There Was the Word
and the Word Was Good

Born from a celestial story: I'm mixed. Half wolf. Half lion.
Constellation so common we bore ourselves with the name.
We've heard this joke before, punch line not even worth pretending.
Dead stars I push around with the tip of my sneaker,
dare I bore myself with myself and my own imagination
of where I come from and how little I regret.
Have learned how to hold back my teeth when I pray.
When I am prostrate before my lover.
He is doing the lord's work.
So am I.

Everything is possible when you learn to walk with a broken limb.
Devastation is described as unexpected climbing. How boring it could end if I weep
at every fallen tree or lay myself down mourning every time I am surprised.
You have never heard me moan. Unless you have. Which you remember.
My teeth remember the resistance of a celestial shoulder.

Someone asked me once why, after my opponent cheated, I was not angry.
I paused to consider whether I had forgotten my rage.
"I won," I laughed a Uranus moon. "I still won."
My ancestors' bones laugh in constellations.
They gave me these teeth. This sharp, sharp ink. This hunger.
I do not regret my birth or my father.
I am not angry or even disappointed
he never taught me what he still does not know
(and even that story is boring too, we've all been in this movie before,
a tale so predictable our teeth fall asleep telling it).

Baby, remember the time I stepped out the screen
to wrap my legs around your waist, your tongue in my mouth?
We made love half-laughing about robbing banks.
Sometimes the jokes we tell are not funny.
Sometimes I kick stars. Sometimes it rains bullets.

Certain scripts always demanding stars and blood and dead and tires that screech

and eyes that follow a collarbone into the horizon
and still feel lips resting on its narrow edge, dipping into the crevice
a perfect yolk and brown sugar melting into an orange sleep
but I can imagine much more entertaining uses for blood than spilling.
Find me when you find yourself swelling.
Maybe even kisses are boring but not when I am properly watered.
Isn't everything a river?
Always leaving. Always here.
I've never been as easy to drown as people think.

Maybe you haven't seen my calves lately, but they're storytellers too, all this walking.
I love and love majestically. Love a majestic man tenderly enough to limp.
Tell me what you know or imagine of courage. I am unafraid of mine.
You have not heard me howl. Roar. Descend from heaven with a clap of thunder.
But you know when I walk into a room.

This warrior body, this heaven been taking names.
My deep-throated east facing caw beckons the sky I come from
to yield its dew, fold sticky-night into boiling.
I am new fresh-born feral, eyes ablaze behind wild-haired navigation.
I do not regret my map my voice my compass my blood,
call caw crow to my bones in breath and they come, unearth and gather, remember their shape.
A low hum, they rumble. It is always now.
The earth's pursed and ready lips come clean into each other.
Erupt into heat and wet so loud we can't wait to write the script.
When did the river learn to run? When did I?

Leapt from heaven into the baptism of my birth:
I breathe natural like nothing is a costume.
Like my blood is my inheritance, belongs to me even when rushing
to the surface of a genius stroke, even when spilling into cosmic joke.
You ever heard blood laugh? When it mocks? When it weeps? When it prays?
When it soars?
Some nights, bones

I Think Your Ancestors Haunt Me

that have forgotten their graves
come, rattle me awake to love
my daughter's hands, the eyes she shares
with her father, and I am God's child
again, heavy with love.

I love a good word, a kept promise,
still frightened of a broken vow.
It is a binding thing, to be God's child;
to have no appetite for lukewarm,
to forgive and forgive,
spiting your own gravity.

To abscond is a slow bleed,
escape a scarlet yoke.
I am folded into a mouth
and chewed, tongue split
down the middle like a family
of orphans, full of hunger and promise.

And it is heavy to love,
to open a body and birth an avalanche
heart only half mine, to carry her
against impossible and climb
until my legs forget to tremble
beneath the weight of prayer and push.

Heavy to recognize
the forever of her and stay
wrapping myself around her rolling
as I am her first skin
and she, the pulp of my disarm,
my one true promise.

What You Know About Delicious?

I want to talk about the way he curves
up a little and how it's enough to make me still
take his calls even though he is probably trifling
and I am not ashamed for you to know that sometimes
when I am quietly half-smiling I am considering
the smoothness of his skin against my lips

and I want to talk about how to make black eyed peas and
greens and cornbread and jambalaya and peanut brittle and
especially how to make twenty dollars feed us for the week
and I want you to smell the rice and the beans and the garlic
getting to know each other in my kitchen while I braid
my hair or my daughter's hair or my homegirl's hair

and I want to fry the potatoes sliced thin like Nana's
and let the onions burn a little and the potatoes too
because I like them a little black in places to feel
the crunch against my teeth I want to talk about how
we danced and drank and laughed and flirted and
danced some more and how the dancing feels

and I want to talk about how round my body is
and how many worlds it contains and how many worlds it builds
always moving in circles and how this is the antidote
the water my ancestors thirsted for this is the antideath
learning what it means to breathe and become alive
and how to live even when the inside curves of cruel feet

fit tight around either side of my neck
weighty opportunists standing on my shoulders asking:
why do you hate yourself isn't this view delicious
and how I shrug them into dust and taste honey and peaches
and pink sea salt the fat kind so the crystals melt slow
as I press them against the back of my teeth

and I want my ancestors to know about all the things
my tongue has learned I want to let it moisturize their bones

and let the fat around my hips move enough
to grease their appetites and let them live in my flesh
and feel this lusty and wet and round body
and call it our inheritance.

Maybe We Are All God's

I wish I knew what to say. I've been so ashamed.
This begging heart that I would not claim.

Kicked it hard in front of company
when it came in loud and stumbling,

knowing I can't afford to look weak,
all empty hands and dirty feet

with some working knowledge of when and how
to unstone a heart or pull a thorn from a crown, and now,

deciding whether I want to, or how to weather;
sometimes leather

is the only way to live,
when there's little left for the well to give

except advice that I don't know how to take
so I'm wondering how many bones to break,

which part of myself to undertake,
wonder if I can regenerate

deciding whether I want to.
Feel like these are some known shoes.

I'm stumbling through on an old path,
realize a labyrinth is just basic math,

and growth happens in spirals too; the vortex of cycles, thought I overflew
when I reached for the sun, the ocean still got her due

and maybe it's true that I love you,
and maybe we'll call this a breakthrough,

but I suspect your breath on my neck
is yet another intoxicant,

I suppose you make me dizzy
I propose that we get busy

pretending we don't have names.
Sometimes I practice forgetting your face

remember mine in its place, say:
pulse, don't race, I brace myself for you not to stay

I make believe it was always this way:
me, humbled in prayer, prostrate.

I find new ways to show devotion to the divine sobriety of my solitude
you might be God, and I'm holy too

and maybe this isn't about you, but me.
You, the shard stuck I don't want to see.

I say: how else do you tame an ocean
but with a mirrored moon, frozen?

A magnet of some magnitude
to mute an ill-conforming mood

or woman in a state of vapor,
whose self defense is second nature

and maybe all trust is reckless
and maybe this love is preface

to a story I already epilogue.
Maybe all my conversations are monologues.

Maybe we are all God's.
Maybe we are all God.

Melt

grandfather smoke billowing into beard
or some other soft disappearance.

key parts of the world are burning
and I'm still checking for missed calls in small and consuming despairs.

maybe the only thing that matters right now
is who I'm standing next to when the flames catch.

but aren't I already burning?
doesn't everything make you want to cry?

yes, we will write poems
even as the embers land on our well loved clothes.

we will cling to each other
tears making maps down our ashen faces

and we will remember love
as we drift.

December Selfies from a Hotel in Massachusetts

it is cold here
dropping into moon;
icicles swell slow
until thick.
my sweater, a tight fire
wanting wood
or vine, dead leaf empires smoking
fever, stiff and steaming
windows. flakes of snow
on my neck, lost moths
burning in pursuit of heat,
swallow into naked
skin and slide, soft into collarbone
cup, holds new wet
in welcome.

it is warm here,
in my heave.

The Things I Could Build

love:
if you are to become past-tense
weight
dead wood
dry cement powder
gravel
dust
plastic sheeting
rusty nails
flathead screws,
i will know what to make of you when you leave.

my stepfather taught me to
dig a fence post
lay a tile
fill the gap with grout
nail the shingle
swing the hammer
coat the brush evenly before dragging it along the wall.

if you are going to lurk, stir near my favorite songs,
your scent circling well-loved cocktail glasses,
you might as well become
my front porch
an expanded master bath
a stair to replace the one that squeaks
a closet door or its hinges.

the love whose copy of The Road i once borrowed: a ceiling fan.
the love who I later saw the film version with: a garbage disposal.

don't these sharp inhales
become a place to live?

next love: you might be an in ground pool
or a raised bed garden
or a fence or a fence Jesus be a fence
we use what we have to build what we need.

the letter e

Meeting called to order at 8:04 a.m.

> who can breathe like this with the two of us in a room together

Agenda reviewed and discussed.

can they hear me wail and pant
do they know this gap is too big to contain
how loud I need to howl

Motion to approve.

I do not know how long I can be polite in company
when the wind in my chest is hurling elephant bones and screaming into
cellars to save me the shame of weeping in public

Do I hear a second?

do you know how long I can hold my breath before I die me neither we
are going to learn together over all this polite behavior I am cracked
porcelain pinching your skin I want to make you bleed
I want you close and closed and how do you hold this in a body all this
whipping wind and water how do I keep from drowning every time you're
in the room

Motion to approve passed unanimously.

don't you feel me aching aren't we each other's phantom limbs

didn't we cut ourselves free have we ever stopped missing us have you ever
stopped missing me
have you ever missed me can you still breathe when I hurl my eyes at your
chest exhaling
doesn't the sun or moon or the letter e or the key of g minor or water or trees
or air make you think of me?

Breakup Poem Number Fifty-Leven

Men who don't love me
I could buy by the barrel.
Those who want the company
of my skin and silence,
I lose count before breakfast.

My last breakup I told him
"I'm glad we caught it early"
like it was a cancer
and not a love.
The one before him, I said
"I really dodged a bullet
this time".

My homegirls never believe me
when I say the men don't love me
because they actually can't imagine
anyone not loving me.
I feel the same way about them,
and ain't that love?
The purest kind?

52

Whales sing to each other.
They call out and know themselves.
Their songs can travel over 3,000 miles.
Whales fall in love.

The whale they call "52" sings at a higher frequency
than all other whales in the word.
They call him "The Loneliest Whale in the World"
because no other whales can hear him.

His species is unknown, but many speculate that he's a hybrid between blue
and fin.
Some think he roams the ocean alone.
Some think he moves among a group of whales, calling out his song,
steady as a metronome.

I move silently through the depths, belly full of unheard song.

Maybe I should weep for Jonah.
Maybe I should wail for the people of Nineveh.
Maybe I should read my freckles until my mouth wants to move again.
Maybe I should stop dragging the dead.

Millions of years ago, whales lived on land.
They walked back into the water.
You know how much an ocean weighs?
Is it heavier than a drowned moan?

One Day We'll All Be Fossil Fuel

I am sure that my breasts are onions sometimes.
Some people are always hungry.
My hunger is a blistered foot, surviving its
circumstances.
I've said I love you and meant it, I've said yes,
Sometimes I wake up with bite marks.
My bite is a warning missing its pin, watching the
line.
All of the hands have left mine callused. I hope you will not mind,
Sometimes my sleep is mangled and gnawed.
My gnaw is a reckless cannibal, willing to work.
I have not always said what was burning in me,
Sometimes I should have said that you would make a beautiful fire.
My fire is its own consolation, becoming a new skin.
I am a knotted ginger root, a garlic clove, a lemon on open skin,
Sometimes you have to burn everything down.
My burn is a ransom note, a list of demands.
I am making new maps, dragging fingertip through ashes and miles
of mouths,
Sometimes I'm supposed to live in half sleep.
My memory is its own consolation, a loose tooth,
dangling.
I understand dragons now, belly all dead wood and dry moss,
Sometimes I shine straight into the shadows.
The line between victim and killer is disappearing.
I am growing new skin, all mirrors in my teeth,
Sometimes I know you cannot love me, you would shatter your own face.
My love is alarmed and arming, loud and leaking.
I cannot expect change, mouth full of your own tail,
Sometimes your name is an ember I have almost forgotten.
My change is a riot, a pulsing trigger, a pointing
finger.
I am a naked forest of ash and parch, peeling away,
Sometimes I want to boil the ocean.
My naked is unafraid, unashamed, and
unapologizing.
I have not always minded the dead,

Sometimes I think forgiveness is an onion.
My forgiveness is a hungry, bloody mouth. A pocket of stones.

How to Reconcile

When my sister and I fought,
our lower backs ached.
We didn't know this happened
to the other sister as well
until we made up,
our roots, aching from the brief separation.

These roots
that tangle and sprout and dive
even breathe as one body,
even different our prayers and
how we picture God's face
the shape of our heaven and bliss
on different flavors my perfect love
a whole octave outside most ears and still:

love
all of its messy knots.

37th and Colorado Boulevard

can you believe
just downwind from the Purina factory
and its rumors of boiled hooves and other tales that frighten children

there are mouths
tongues and teeth and throats
conspiring in sound
telling stories

for instance:
do you know
at Bethsaida temple church
my grandmother has played the piano for 35 years
and has played there even as recently as this morning?

that I learned to sing his eye is on the sparrow
right there in the shadow of the oil refinery's glowing lights and towers?

Saturday Morning in the Garden

Me and this sun been knowing each other for a long time. The sun remembers when I was a baby. The sun remembers when I was born. We embrace and swallow each other. I cannot always tell us apart. I remember when the sun was little. I remember when the sun was born. "Look what we made," we laugh toothlessly at the mess before and behind us. The throes of tornado and rock we call seed and love and ourselves and home. We transform everything we touch.

Always Carry a Shovel

I have remembered after having forgotten
which lands are mine
which fields I left burning
without a single longing to become salt.
I am learning to leave home.

I am remembering myself
the compass in my belly
the scythe in my throat
walking direct into the sunrise singing my name my God my child
a tune I am remembering.
I am learning to find home.

Yes, I have remembered myself
after having forgotten
caught in a grasp of bramble and thistle who whisper
to me of lands I have already charted
the broken promises of lands I have escaped.
Lands I have reclaimed bones from.
I am remembering I am home.

Empty Nesting

I do not owe you
my children
any children
in spite
of these hips, wider even
than the gap between
my two front teeth,
perhaps more narrow
than the gap between me
and your imagination of me,
my bosom, heavy
and milkless.
The weight.
The too much.
The never enough.
The just shy.
The almost.
The miracles.
The sleepless sweat.
The shrink.
The collapse.
I gave myself (to) one child.
I did not do it for you.

How the Fool Survives

aren't I a master of laughter?
don't I don a dance when it suits me
like armor, a second skin or third?
haven't I had to keep them laughing to keep from killing me all this time?
aren't I a body of hungry wolves?
aren't I ready to eat?

aren't I a spear?
don't I carry a mask as a weapon in one hand?
doesn't it cut like a scythe?
don't we cull?
don't we prune?
isn't it curing to be naked in the sun?

aren't we thorough in our breath?
don't we love the song of the wind and sweet crickets?
aren't they still heard singing in the morning?
don't their music offer some kind of shelter?
aren't I sharp enough to find them through the grass?
isn't our song the same?

do you hear that?
the hum so howl it vibrates?
don't it make you dance?

The World Ends and Ends

me & my cousin laughing about the perfect shade thrown by old ladies:
    "i like how you had your hair yesterday."
    "that dress don't leave much to the imagination."
    "did you mean to go that short?"
    "you know what's a better color for you?"

her friend interjects, says shade from old men hits harder.

my cousin says we wouldn't know. we don't have any old men in our family.
my cousin is in town for a funeral. again.
we have learned to mourn.
we have learned to laugh and cry in a single sentence.

---

my cousin's father died days before her birthday.
her birthday. she wants me to hear her freestyle.
she left rehab to come to the funeral.
she is afraid to rap for me because i'm a serious poet, she says.
i tell her i can pull up instrumentals on my phone.
i step outside with her while she smokes her cigarette and raps.
she's leaving a voicemail for someone i don't know.
someone she says owes her money.
her freestyle is mostly about the debt she is trying to collect.
she reminds him that she knows where his momma stays.
her language is sharp.
she blushes when two old white ladies walk past looking shocked.
we look at each other and laugh like when we were little girls.
she finds her rhythm again.
"over there (she is pointing) is where my granny got her first DUI"
and over there (she is pointing again) is where i got my first DUI"
her birthday
her daddy just died
her birthday
the bar has cut her off
her birthday
she loves everyone
except that MF whose name i don't know

she wipes her face and says we not doin this today
i say go ahead and cry cousin
she asks me to take her to get weed so she can be happy again
my cousin is a language i understand
i say no
she snatches drinks from the table and they are half gone before we can stop her
she laughs
she think she slick
she is
slippery as age and sobriety
we got good calluses for grip
we hold each other
in prayer
in hope
in resignation
in memory
i hug my cousin, say she is still magnificent and i still see her
i hug her son, her nephew, say she wasn't always like this

---

me & my cousins stayed up late in my auntie's basement
practicing our dance routines
Summer the choreographer
Tammy the ballerina
me & Raven the youngest mostly doing what they said
but put our own spin on the snake shaking our shapeless hips
pinched our nostrils together and sucked them in while we did the cabbage patch
took turns dancing in the circle shouting "go, go, go"
until it was "go Suzi, go Suzi, go, go, go Suzi" and I would get shy
and say I didn't want to dance no more
and sometimes we could hear the grown folks yelling at each other upstairs
but we could turn the music up and keep dancing
playing Janet Jackson until the tape warped
playing Whitney Houston until the tape warped
until somebody yelled for us to shut up and go to bed
and don't-make-me-come-down-these-stairs

we laugh and cry in a single sentence
we lose and find our rhythm in a single bar
we live while the world ends and ends and ends

Sing Over the Bones

and this is what we call
the black girl blues
ain't called it depression
so much as Tuesday
when we forget the promise
of Saturday night sweat
and Sunday morning song
when we forget to call tomorrow holy
'cause it's another hill to climb
when today leaves bruises
catches round our throats
and leaves our voices whispers
when we forget to rebuke madness
and call it the truth
we must remember
to say to ourselves:

You are not crazy. Resist when they snap at you
to stretch your scabbed skin back over your bones.
You will grow it anew every time. If your veins are easy
to see this does not mean that you are easy to kill, only
that your life is impossible to ignore. You are a bleeding
sun. When the calluses form, tear your skin from its meat,
peel yourself open and let them smell the fruit of you, spill
into every mouth that speaks your name, stain their fingers
you. You, magnificent point of light, a swallowing supernova.
You are hammer and pickax, bellyful of lava, you are a forever
thing. When dark has forgotten it's own weakness, you are
flame, dancing it into hush. You are a blistering miracle, sun and
sand tangled into indistinguishable horizon. Hum, and the earth
will keep on course, you song, you lovely, you yes, you fiery stone
mouth, you fleshy mirror, you pulpy always, you marvelous in your
questing, glorious in pursuit of humble corners, you worship, you
God-child, you Queen of Margins and handwritten notes. There is
nothing wrong with you. You are a unicorn in a herd of goldfish
muddying the pond, and no one has learned yet to sing your name.
You, star. You, stone. You, shine. You, always. You, inextinguishable.

You, perfect.
You, perfect.

Dark Humor

you know how my hips
have never forgotten the drum?

you know the way my voice
sounds like a conjured Grandmother?

you know how I write
poems like invocations, right?

you know how my spirit never sleeps?
how we laugh at our own temporary blood?

and oh, sweet Lord,
how we laugh!

how buckets of glass leap from our heads, thrown back and open,
how we spill sharp, choking out the swallowed stingers;

how we dance until our feet blister and open,
knowing the stains will tell the story of our movement;

we super magic, we beloved immortal,
even our echoes got knuckles;

listen, in the canyons, over the ocean crashing,
our ancestors stay chanting:

we in here.
we still here.
we been here.
we stay here.
we survived.
we survived.
we survived.

beloved

beloved:
break. open and rest.

unhide what golden sun spills
when you weep into the wound,
uncovered.

you have never been alone.
you are always alone.
you have been found.

you will always be sought and seen
coiled into spiral,
curled into fist,
calmed into open.

even the ocean floor
smiles and knows your face,
returning you back to you
like a sweet moon.

beloved
i sing to myself

i lean into the vortex the whirlpool the black hole the hurricane's eye
the open mouth the edge of the universe the sinking clouds i sing

beloved:
i know your name.

How to Say Goodbye

Dear Grief,

with your precious damp
traipsing muddy footprints
all through the house,
your shivering lilac fingertips,

here:
bring your gravity,
your well-earned weight, and sip.
I sweetened your tea with honey,
shaved the cinnamon. picked and
roasted the dandelions with
my own two hands, brewed it
for you and this pit in my chest.

this stew, all cumin warm carrot,
all ginger sweet thick, is for you alone.

have a bath, wise one.
it is drawn and salted,
oiled and flowered, heated
near to boiling.

when you are warm, fed,
clean, and freshly robed,
I will watch you walk away,
the sun yellow against your back.

What We Make of Mud

1. I Do Not Know How Many People it Has Taken to Make Me.

My uncle, who is known to bring laughter,
once told me a story about my great-grandmother,
how she worked alongside her husband in the fields
with a swollen belly until she went into labor,
at which point she waddled into the house,
gave birth to their baby, and had supper on the table
when her husband came inside that evening.
I thought this exaggeration of my uncle's was hilarious
until I learned that this story is true,
that I am made of such stories.

My grandmother, who remembers all the stories,
once told me about her Great Aunt Song,
of the Blackfoot tribe, who was kidnapped
and sold into slavery as a teenaged girl.
Aunt Song became a cautionary tale in our family
because of her insubordination
and the frequent beatings that she suffered.
She never forgot that she was free as milkweed,
never bundled her pride in a basket of reeds
and sent it down the river for a better life,
never apologized for the strength in her jaw,
Aunt Song never broke.

My great-grandmother on my father's side
was raised to pass for white, but she fell in love with the milkman,
passing secret letters in the milk box until they finally eloped.
They raised eleven children during the depression.
Pulled frozen turnips from the ground one hard
and hungry winter, made it a meal.
Taught all of them to read and write poetry,
to play the piano, and to sing.
We are still a family of music makers,
we are mouths full of song and survive.

My great-great-grandmother
on my mother's side
lost her husband suddenly to a fever
when their son was still new in the world.
She strapped her baby to her hip,
took to the cotton fields in Tennessee
until her weathered hands worked their way
to pull potatoes from a cold Colorado welcome.
We have called it home ever since.

My mother's mother, a church-going woman
(whose mother, I hear, used to read
tea leaves in the parlor),
raised seven children
with needle and thread,
with wooden spoons and batter,
calling the corners and stitching them together,
folding the rhubarb in with the sugar.
We are always making something beautiful
out of what we can grow.

My grandmother on my father's side,
has taught me nearly everything I know.
Grandmothers, all of them, will live
always, in the mud of my flesh
and the earth of my bones.
We are forever.

2. We Still Remember How to Make Things.

The first storytellers were women.
Gathered 'round steaming cauldrons,
grinding mortar and pestle,
the medicine makers,
the kitchen witches,
the magic movers,
the balm brewers,

the mud women,
combing the earth for seeds to pass on to their daughters.

They found that cardamom, native to the evergreen forests in India,
is good to clean the blood, heal the mouth and throat, and lift depression.
The best secret a mother might whisper to her daughter
the night before she marries is that the spicy, citrus seed
is a well-respected aphrodisiac and will surely
bring her husband to task.

The mud women know all about cinnamon, popular since ancient Egypt
for treating coughs and aches, and while our ancestors
might not have called it anti-microbial, they knew good medicine
when they smelled it.

If you've ever sipped on tea made from ginger root,
you know it will save your life in winter.
The mud women know this, too,
and how thyme helps us to breathe,
and how garlic cleans the blood
and everything else with it.

Mud women know these things,
cultivating cures at kitchen tables
and call it dinner,

you can call them old wives' tales
if you want to, but we all come to the day
when we know our grandmother
was right.

3. A Song of Gratitude

Thank you for the dirt
that has become my family.

Thank you for the sweet air,

crisp as an ironed dress on Sunday morning.

Thank you for the trees,
huddled close in pastures, whispering secrets like children under a table.

Thank you for the hovering hummingbirds,
for the honeybees, for the night's lulling crickets.

Thank you for my quiet hands,
for the story of my new eyes.

Thank you for teaching my feet
to sing the name of my mother's home until it is mine also.

4. We Have Not Forgotten How to Dig.

I come from a long line of mighty women.
Women who remember. Women who tell.
Women who put their hands in the mud,
divining truth and sweeping shadows.

I am still learning from my ancestors;
listen when they whisper
over a pot of black-eyed peas
"drop a little peanut butter in it, baby",

feel them stir in my cells and ask for water,
for lemon and cayenne,
taught me that coconut oil is as good for the hair
as it is for the elbows and door hinges,

know that it is they who taught me
that a little apple cider vinegar and honey
cures all but broken bones and hurt feelings,
(but they got something for all of that, too).

We all come from something bigger, some root

that reminds us we were alive before our memory
began to frame the story. And we all leave something behind,
if only our bones, we all return as seed.

I plant my bare feet in the mud whenever I can.
I call it home.

We Sang Ourselves Free

We didn't always know we would win. Just that we would do whatever we had to in order to get free. We used to sing softly to each other, to our selves, hum low under our breath to remember our voices in places we were unwelcome. We danced in secret. We laughed silently across rooms, taking our quiet joys and tucking them into our pockets like perfumed handkerchiefs we could smell later when we needed to remember.

Our foremothers and forefathers built a bridge of sound and hope that only a few could hear. We heard their call from the heavens, though, and we answered them all, we answered becoming flesh and voice and song. If you listen closely enough, you will know how beautiful we are. Someone tried to stop their music. The love they found each other in. Tried to turn them into silence, as if they could ever be less than furious messengers of a love lived out loud. Everything we do is song. We are a dance, unsilenceable.

One day, we saw the first rose bloom in years when we sang the low notes we'd been singing since before time had a name. We got louder. More people joined in the song and the grasses awoke from their slumber. The wolves came and sat at our feet, weeping. The rains came down and the trees remembered us. We began again and knew, we knew God was listening.

And the rains came the way the come. Slow and sweet at first, washing the old ash and dust to the rivers. Then again there were rivers where we washed our hands and feet. Where we washed each other's hair. Where we sang our old songs and the earth heard, answering in heather and pine. And she answered in the day's harvest, yellows spiraling into violets, sweets wrapping themselves in spicy oranges and fuchsias tumbling over each other to embrace the sour and soft fruit of each other.

We ate and grew fat again. We all fell madly in love and raised perfect children. The sort of perfect that brought us into each day, laughing. We grinned rich as noonday, each of us carrying the songs and teaching them to the children, how to stretch a note all the way into fingertips until the trees begin to sway.

You feel that? We said to each other, our hairs standing to answer the electric air.

Yes. We all answered.

Yes.

The First Law of Thermodynamics Says I Live Forever

ain't it wild that we still dance?
that people have the nerve to be entertained by our movement?
they don't play chess, i guess, don't know how small movements change a game.
how unstoppable this climb. how unkillable this smile.

don't you know i been here before?
will be here after?
that i am an exploded sun, breathing?
see? it's funny. how they think we die.

Suzi Q. Smith is an award-winning artist, activist, and educator who lives in Denver, Colorado. She has been performing poetry throughout the United States for over a decade.

Performing across the U.S. for over a decade, she has shared stages with Nikki Giovanni, the late Gil Scott Heron, and many more. Her poems have appeared in *Union Station Magazine, Suspect Press, La Palabra, Muzzle Magazine, Malpais Review, The Pedestal, The Los Angeles Journal, Denver Syntax, Word is Bond, The Peralta Press, Yellow Chair Review,* and in the anthologies *The Mutiny Info Reader, Diverse-City, His Rib: Anthology of Women,* and *In Our Own Words,* and her chapbook collection of poems, *Thirteen Descansos,* was published by Penmanship Books. She co-wrote the dramatic productions *How I Got Over: Journeys in Verse* and *Where We Are From: Freedom is a Constant Struggle.*

Suzi Q. has also worked extensively as an activist with civil rights organizations, victims advocate organizations, arts organizations, peace organizations, hospitals, prisons, and more. She was the founding Slammaster of Denver's Slam Nuba, and she spent 12 years in the poetry slam arena as a coach, organizer, and performer. In addition, she has worked extensively with youth, serving as a Teaching Artist with Youth On Record, and as a coach of Denver Minor Disturbance Youth Poetry Slam, resulting in two international championships. Currently, Suzi Q. is at work on her next collection while she continues to teach Creative Writing.

www.ingramcontent.com/pod-product-compliance
Lightning Source LLC
Chambersburg PA
CBHW021153090426

42740CB00008B/1072